Singing
A Technical Guide

By Kathryn Kasper

Introduction

This book can be used together with the YouTube posts under Kathryn Kasper or kaspervocalmethod.

This is a book to help you learn how to sing. It is practical for teachers of singing, professional as well as amateur singers, pop soloists and choir singers. It is the book I wish I had when I began to study singing. It has taken me over 50 years of teaching to reduce to these few pages what we need to do when we sing.

It is not meant to be read like a novel. It is important to apply the information as you read. We all have a voice, but we need to learn how to use it to its greatest potential. It may also be helpful to watch the exercises as presented on my YouTube posts. The chapters of this book mainly follow the order of the videos.

There is a lot of repetition of information from chapter to chapter, but repetition is how we learn. As a teacher of voice, if I am unwilling to repeat the same basic information at each lesson, always a bit differently and without getting impatient, I am not a good teacher.

An athlete or dancer repeats the same movements every day. We, singers, need to pattern ourselves after an athlete. They learn to use the correct muscles to execute a movement. An athlete relies on muscle memory, and we need to do the same, but first, what muscles do we use?

After you have digested the first four chapters, it is perfectly fine to skip around. There are often two chapters with the same basic information, only explained a bit differently. Since we all learn differently, feel free to find what helps you the most. There are exercises at the end of many chapters. Repeat them. Muscle memory is essential.

This book presents the total system used while singing classical, Broadway, or popular music. It is complex, but not difficult to learn with guidance. This book and the videos are your guides.

Dedication

I would like to dedicate this book to the hundreds of students I have taught in the last fifty some years. I have learned something from each one of them and I thank them all.

About the Author

Kathryn Dick Kasper was born in Lima Ohio in 1940, moving to Eastern Montana with her Mennonite pastor family at the age of two. She completed grade school in a one room schoolhouse and one year of high school in Richey Montana. There was always music in the home. The children were lined up, sitting on the floor, given sheet music, always singing four parts. Handel's Hallelujah Chorus was a favorite.

When the family increased in size to eight children, the family moved to Winton California. After three years at Livingston High School she followed her older brother to Bethel College in North Newton Kansas where, for the first time she attended formal music classes and took voice lessons. Within three weeks of graduating four years later with a Music Education degree she married Arlo Kasper. They have been married for 63 years.

After having two children, Rachel and Michael, she received her Master of Music in Voice from Wichita State University. Receiving a Fulbright to study in Germany and with Arlo's first Sabbatical from Bethel College, the family moved to Wiesbaden Germany for two years. The following 30 plus years were spent teaching voice, mainly at Bethel College. Arlo and Kathryn prepared many theater productions, both acting themselves and preparing student productions. Kathryn presented a formal recital every year.

After retiring in 2006 and receiving a Fulbright to work at the UniNorte Opera Company in Asuncion Paraguay she and Arlo moved to Asuncion. They have lived in Asuncion for twenty years, always returning to North Newton Kansas for December through February, the summer school break in Paraguay. One highlight during this time was her part in preparation of the 540 voice choir for the Pope Francis visit to the country in 2015.

Kathryn has taught at all of the Bachelor music programs in the country and continues to teach with a University program and privately. She and Arlo have produced operas, musicals and theater reviews throughout these years. They have contributed greatly to the cultural life of Paraguay.

Table of Contents

Chapter 1 1

Chapter 2 5

Chapter 3 8

Chapter 4 11

Chapter 5 13

Chapter 6 16

Chapter 7 19

Chapter 8 21

Chapter 9 23

Chapter 10 26

Chapter 11 28

Chapter 12 30

Chapter 13 33

Chapter 14 35

Chapter 15 37

Chapter 16 40

Chapter 17 42

Chapter 18 44

Chapter 19 46

Chapter 1

Inhalation and Support for Singers

Learning to sing is like learning to play a sport. Repetition is the key factor in both. How many times does a basketball or soccer player repeat the same move before doing it correctly? Before it becomes a habit? Hundreds? Maybe even thousands of times.

Singing requires the same disciplined approach. We need to learn which muscles to use and which not to use.

Stating the obvious, singing is inextricably linked with breathing. Most people know that when we inhale, our lungs expand to take in air. But the real hero in breathing and supporting sound is the diaphragm. To understand healthy inhalation and support, we need to understand how the diaphragm functions.

The diaphragm is one of the largest muscles in the body, separating the thorax, or chest, from the abdominal area. Above the diaphragm are the lungs and heart. Below the diaphragm are the stomach and many internal organs, along with the intestines. If you touch the upper abdomen right below the sternum and cough, you can feel the diaphragm tense.

The diaphragm has the form of an upside-down bowl. The bottom edges of the diaphragm connect to the ribs and spine. When we inhale, the bowl flattens slightly, which expands the ribs. Also aiding in this expansion are the external intercostals, the muscles between the ribs.

Let us look at the anatomy of breathing from top to bottom, beginning with the mouth. Ideally, we inhale mainly through the mouth for singing. Nose breathing is slow and noisy. When we inhale for singing, we need to do it rapidly and silently. We may take in some air through the nose, but mostly we inhale through the mouth.

The second part is the throat. If we do not open the throat when inhaling, we hear a lot of noise. We open the throat by widening the tongue. This is explained more completely in Chapter 3. When both the mouth and throat are open, the air can enter silently. After inhaling, the lungs have a layer of new air directly above the diaphragm. This is the air we use when singing.

The diaphragm and the ribs work together to enlarge the lungs, allowing the air to enter. The first muscular movement is the lowering of the diaphragm. The diaphragm pushes down slightly onto the internal organs to make more space above it, allowing the lungs to lengthen and air to enter.

As the diaphragm flattens, the ribs expand. Aiding in this movement are the external intercostals, the outer layer of muscles between the ribs. Now the ribs are wider at the sides and back.

Air always goes where there is less pressure. We do not inhale air. We lower the diaphragm and open the ribs on the sides and back, and the air comes in. The mouth is open, the throat is open, and the air enters. By lowering the diaphragm and expanding the ribs, we create a partial vacuum in the lungs, and the air automatically enters the lower lungs.

Now, how do we get the air out? We raise the abdominal muscles above the belly button with a movement inward and upward. This presses the internal organs more firmly against the diaphragm, pressing the diaphragm up against the lungs. The newly inhaled air is now under more pressure.

The control of the exhalation is due to two points of resistance: the abdominals pushing up and the external intercostals resisting the upward movement. It is important to maintain the expansion of the ribs as we sing. The air goes out in a controlled manner.

Do not tense the abdominal muscles. Simply move them inward and upward. They need to remain flexible. If the abdominal muscles are tense, the throat will be tense. If the throat is relaxed, the abdominal muscles will relax, and the throat will close. The system is alert. The system is open and remains open while singing.

Do not think of pushing the air out. The air goes out because it is under more pressure than the air outside the body. It is a complex system that relies on the open mouth, open throat, and the movement of the ribs and diaphragm.

Exercises to Maintain the Core in the Body

Sit-ups

Sing while doing them.

Modified Sit-ups

a.   Sit sideways in a chair with one hand holding the back of the chair. Raise your legs. Lean back and do sit-ups while singing.

b.   While sitting on the front edge of a chair, lean back and sit up while singing.

Wall Exercise

Stand with your back flat against a wall. Bend your knees and press the small of your back against the wall. Sing. When comfortable with the position, step away from the wall, keeping your back as close as possible to the position it had when against the wall. Sing. Repeat.

YouTube Reference

"The Movements of the Diaphragm" https://youtu.be/Y0W_sueD3Gc

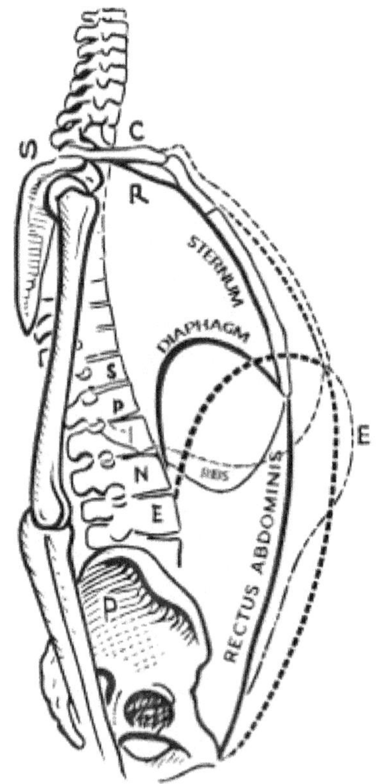

S
C
R
STERNUM
DIAPHAGM
S
P
I
N
E
RIBS
RECTUS ABDOMINIS
E
P

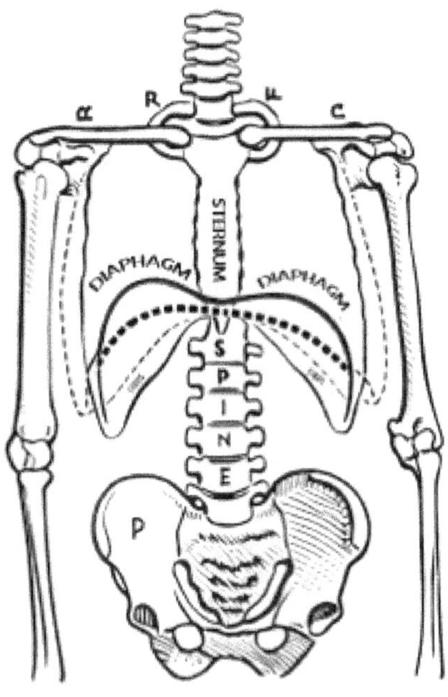

R
R
L
C
STERNUM
DIAPHAGM
DIAPHAGM
S
P
I
N
E
P

Chapter 2

The Lungs, Diaphragm, and Ribs and How to Maintain Support as We Sing

The structure of the thorax, or chest, is created by the ribs. Inside the ribs are the lungs and heart.

Let us first consider the lungs specifically. The lungs do not have any muscles. They are completely passive. They respond only to the movements of the ribs and diaphragm. The lungs are connected to the ribs in the front, sides, and back and to the diaphragm at the bottom. They are also connected to the spine in the back. Only by moving the ribs and diaphragm do we inhale and exhale.

When we are sitting or in a passive position, the movements of the ribs and diaphragm are so small that we are not aware of them. However, when we sing, the movements are larger and stronger.

As the ribs expand, the lungs become wider. As we lower the diaphragm, the lungs become longer. The size of the lungs is determined by the position of the ribs and diaphragm.

If we expand the ribs high in the chest, the air enters only to that level. The upper lungs have expanded. To exhale, we collapse those ribs and the air goes out. This is not helpful while singing. There is no control over the air. The throat will close.

When we inhale through the mouth and the open throat, the lower ribs automatically expand with the aid of the external intercostal muscles. These are the muscles between the ribs. This new air enters low in the lungs, directly above the diaphragm. The lungs are now wider and longer.

To exhale, or to begin singing, we raise the upper abdominals, those muscles above the belly button. This movement pushes the internal organs more firmly against the diaphragm.

These two systems work in opposition to each other, together putting the air under pressure. The air goes out as a result of this pressure. We do not exhale; we let these two opposing systems do the work.

Do not think of relaxing the diaphragm when inhaling. Open the ribs and raise the upper abdominals. We are ready to sing.

We need to maintain the position of inhalation while singing. The ribs are expanded, and the upper abdominals are raised. The system is not rigid. It is flexible.

Exercises for Maintaining Support

The first two exercises are a repeat from Chapter 1.

Sit-ups

These can be done on the floor or on a chair.

a. Sit sideways in a chair, legs extended. Hold on to the back of the chair for security. Do sit-ups while singing an exercise or phrase.
b. While sitting on the front edge of a chair, extend your legs forward. Lean back and do sit-ups while singing.

Wall Exercise

Stand against a wall. Bend your knees and push the small of your back against the wall. The head should not be touching the wall. Now sing an exercise or a phrase of a song. When familiar with the position, step away from the wall, keeping the posture you had while leaning against it.

Rib Expansion Awareness

If you are having trouble feeling the expansion of the ribs, bend forward slightly at the waist. Now inhale. You can easily feel the expansion. Sing a phrase in that position. Gradually stand upright while singing. If you lose the expansion, bend forward again and repeat until the expansion feels secure and open.

Arm Circles

Stand with your arms extended sideways. Slowly draw circles with your hands while singing. Correct posture is very important while singing. The upper chest needs to feel forward and up, not caved in. The upper back is expanded. This exercise aids in obtaining correct posture.

Knee Bends

Bend your knees while singing, maintaining the expanded and raised chest and the open back.

Chapter 3

The Larynx, Tongue, and the Pharynx

The vocal tract is lined at the bottom and back by the larynx, the tongue, and the pharynx.

Let us begin with the larynx. The larynx is composed of a series of cartilages, the largest being the thyroid cartilage. Cartilage is flexible, like the tip of the nose. There are no bones in this part of the anatomy.

The larynx sits at the top of the trachea and is connected to the trachea by a specially formed ring called the cricoid. The rocking movement between the larynx and the cricoid cartilage aids in the changing of pitches. The vocal chords extend from the thyroid cartilage, behind the Adam's apple, backward to the two arytenoid cartilages. As the pitch ascends, the arytenoid cartilages move back and the chords, or vocal folds, become longer and thinner. All of these movements are controlled by muscles within the thyroid cartilage. You can find more information on the internet relating to this complex coordination.

The larynx has no strength of its own. It relies on the muscles that connect it to the tongue, hyoid bone, and pharynx for stability. To find your larynx, touch your Adam's apple. This is the front of the larynx. With your thumb and first finger, move to the sides of the larynx and swallow. The larynx moves up and down. Now open your mouth and inhale. The larynx is now a little wider. By lowering the larynx, we lengthen the vocal tract slightly.

The tongue is composed of many muscles, many of which affect what happens within the larynx. When at rest, the tip of the tongue touches behind the upper tips of the lower front teeth. While singing, it widens against the molars. Behind the molars, the tongue widens further. These posterior muscles that widen the tongue are connected to the larynx and aid in maintaining an open structure in the throat. It may be useful to think of these muscles as two vertical pins that connect the tongue and larynx and hold the throat open.

The third part is the pharynx. It is the back wall of the throat. If you have a sore throat, the pharynx is infected. The pharynx extends upward from behind the larynx to behind the uvula and soft palate. Behind the pharynx is the spine. The pharynx can be moved only by moving the spine.

The Alexander Technique is very useful when we deal with the pharynx. With this technique, we move the spine and as a result, the pharynx, slightly backward while raising the top of the head. The chin needs to remain level. This gives the singer or speaker more space between the larynx and the pharynx. This space enables the singer to have a fuller, easier voice with more of the fundamental. We will learn more about this concept in future chapters.

Exercise

Sing a pitch while alternating between the expanded pharynx using the Alexander Technique and the relaxed pharynx. Record your voice. Do not breathe between the two sounds. Repeat. This is the beginning of the fundamental.

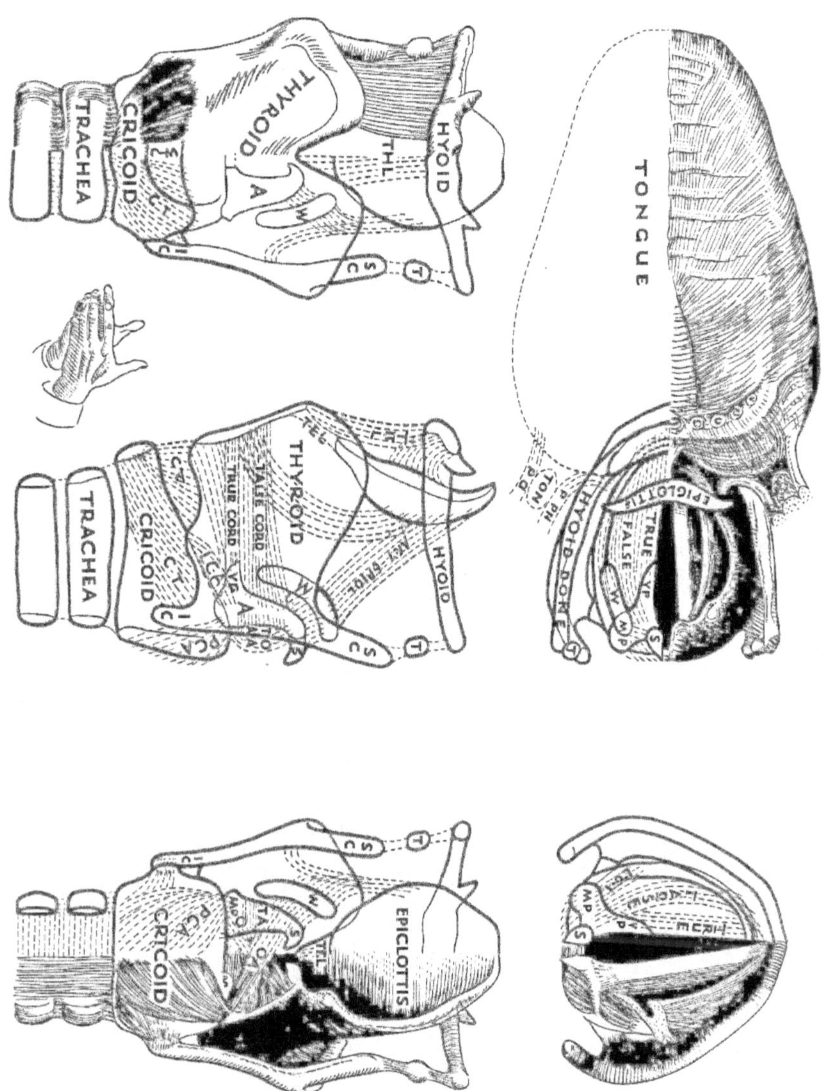

TRACHEA
CRICOID
THYROID
HYOID
THL
TONGUE
THYROID
TRACHEA
CRICOID
FALSE CORD
TRUE CORD
HYOID
TONGUE
EPIGLOTTIS
TRUE
FALSE
HYOID DORS
CRICOID
PCA
EPIGLOTTIS
THL

Chapter 4

The Parts Lining the Vocal Tract

In Chapter 3, I introduced the lower part of the vocal tract: the larynx, the tongue, and the pharynx. In this chapter, I will introduce the other parts that line the vocal tract.

The lips are the most frontal part of the vocal tract. They are flexible. They can widen, flatten, tense, and protrude. The ideal form is an oval with a bit of a frontal extension. They should not be tense. With the extension of the lips, we lengthen the vocal tract slightly.

The hard palate is behind the top teeth and at the top of the frontal oral cavity. It is not flexible. To find it, touch the top front teeth with the tip of your tongue. Move the tongue back along the palate until you hear and feel a click. The soft tissue that clicks is the soft palate. An extension of it is the uvula. As a child, we called it the little tongue.

The soft palate and uvula are flexible. How we use these parts when singing is a great topic of discussion among students and teachers of singing.

Many singers are taught to raise the soft palate and feel an inside smile, creating a cavern directly behind the hard palate. By creating this space, we hear a great deal of resonance inside the mouth. The shape inside is a rectangle, wider than tall.

I have taught this form in the past. I will discuss the soft palate and uvula in detail in future chapters.

The cheeks line the sides of the vocal tract. They should remain relaxed while singing.

The movement of the jaw up and down changes the space inside the oral cavity. Normally, the jaw lowers as the pitch ascends.

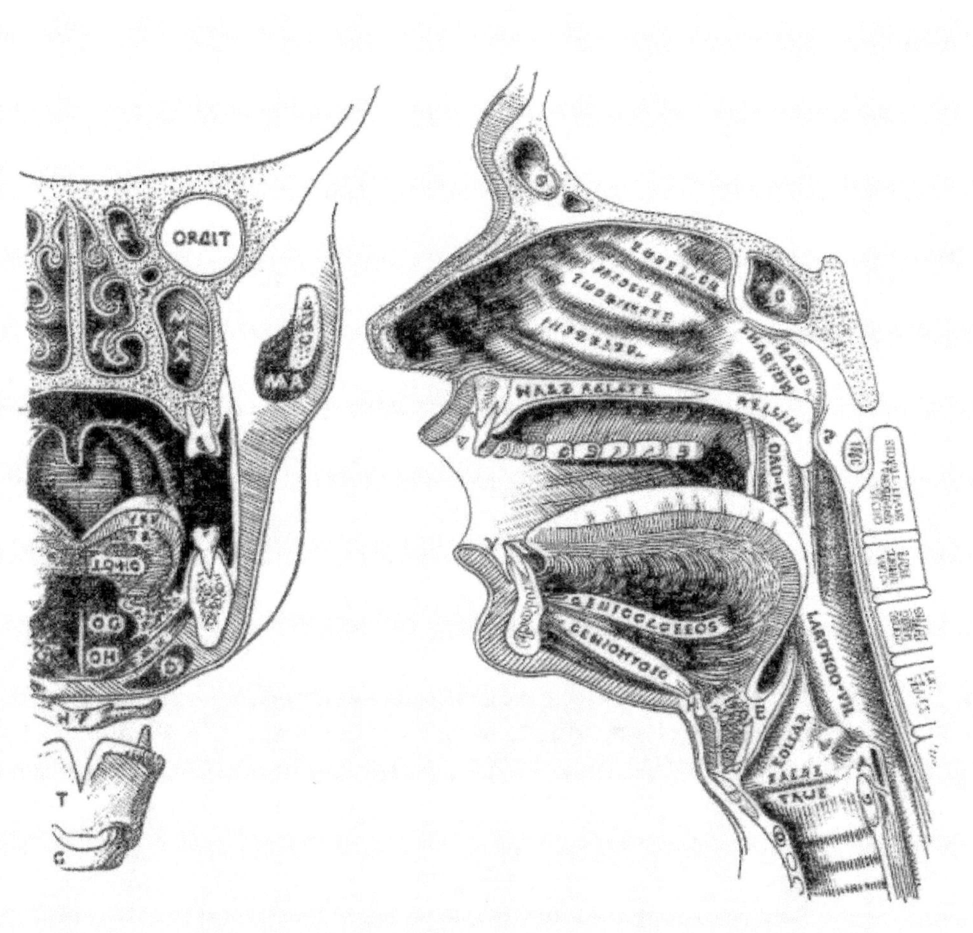

ORBIT
HARD PALATE
SOFT PALATE
GENIOGLOSSUS
GENIOHYOID
LARYNGO-PHA
EPIGLOTTIS

Chapter 5

The First and Second Harmonics or The Fundamental and Vowels

When we think of projecting the voice, we often think we need to push the voice out. Usually, while pushing the voice, we tense the larynx and tighten the abdominal muscles. We need to change what we do to project the voice.

The projection of the voice has two components: The fundamental pitch and the vowels and consonants.

The fundamental pitch is created at the level of the vocal chords. First, let us find out where that fundamental is. If we begin with a vocal fry, we can feel the vibration of the chords deep in the larynx. Now open the throat by widening the tongue, continuing to make a vocal sound. (This might be thought of as a monster voice.) Continue opening the throat by moving the spine and pharynx backward. Now change to a pitch without stopping the sound. Keeping the throat open, raise the pitch like a siren, up and down.

If we look into a mirror as we do the siren, the pharynx and the uvula should remain in view. If the tongue moves up, begin again, repeating until the tongue remains in its low position. We are learning to use the correct muscles. Remember, repetition is the key to all sports, and singing is a sport. Repeat, repeat, repeat.

Now we have the basis of the fundamental. It is a sound that begins in the larynx and does not change its original position as the pitch goes up and down. This sound does not have a vowel. It is an uh [ʌ]. When a symbol is between two brackets, it is a symbol using the International Phonetic Alphabet, IPA. These symbols are explained in depth in Chapter 15.

The vowels and consonants are created with the tongue and lips. Remember, the form of the lips is an oval, sometimes called a fish mouth.

First, try going from the uh [ɑ] to an ah [ɑ]. As we change to the [ɑ], the tongue must remain low in the back but move forward, pressing a bit more against the lower front teeth. The jaw will lower slightly. Do a siren with the [ɑ], low to high to low. The uvula and pharynx must remain in view.

Return to the fundamental uh [ʌ], now moving to the open o [ɔ]. We sing mostly the open o, using the closed o mainly in diphthongs. The lips are round and protrude slightly. They are not tense. The tongue remains low in the back. Do a siren with the [ɔ], low to high to low. The uvula and pharynx must remain in view.

The [i] vowel is a bit different, as the sides of the tongue rise to touch the upper molars. Move the tongue along the molars to the front until the sound of the [i] is projected. The connection to the teeth will be further back on the tongue. The pharynx cannot be seen while executing an [i]. See the exercise at the end of the chapter.

This resonance of the vowels we will call the second harmonic. The words will be projected if we begin with the fundamental. Think of the words sounding only in front of the lips, not inside the mouth. The less clearly we hear the words inside our mouths, the clearer they are to the listener. Do not listen to the voice via the Eustachian tubes. These are the tubes that connect the inner ear to the throat.

The vocal tract is open, the uvula is down, and the air and sound move out past the lips. The frontal part of the tongue and the lips create the words. The back of the tongue moves but remains low.

Exercises

1. If we hear the initial sound on the soft or hard palate, the tongue is raised in the back. This is a lovely sound inside our mouths, but not a sound the public wants to hear.

These might be the problems:

    a. You are pushing the air out. Return to Chapters 1 and 2.

    b. The pharynx is not sufficiently back and open and, as a result, lacks the fundamental.

2. Do some alternate sit-ups. Go back to the swallow to secure the fundamental. Move the spine slightly back. Lower the uvula.

3. Many people have problems with the [i]. Open the mouth into an oval. Without moving the jaw, move the tongue from an [ʌ] to an [i]. Repeat the movement until the tongue moves sufficiently forward and the vowel projects. The middle part of the tongue will touch the upper molars at the beginning of the [i], and as the tongue moves to a more frontal position, the connection to the upper molars will shift toward the posterior of the tongue.

4. To help in the projection of the vowels and consonants, it can be useful to use a couple of aids:

    a. Put the palms of your hands on your cheeks. As you open your mouth, the palms move inward. The fingers are beside the ears, but away from them. Sing. The sound you hear is close to the sound the public hears.

    b. Put your index fingers on each side of your mouth. Sing. You will hear a different quality of sound, closer to the sound the public hears.

    c. Place your index finger under your nose, all fingers extended. Sing. The voice projects directly out of the mouth. The form of the vocal tract is correct.

Chapter 6

Resonance

We all want resonance in our voice because with resonance, the voice projects and has quality. There are many different schools of thought as to how to gain resonance in the singing voice, and I have taught most of them in my over 50 years of teaching.

In a voice class while studying for my doctorate, my teacher said to me that he didn't hear much resonance in my voice. He didn't offer any advice as to how to alleviate the problem. I left the class very discouraged. Not being a slacker, I worked on hearing more resonance in my voice. I pushed the sound into the frontal masque, obtaining a lot of resonance inside my mouth and nasal passages. At the next lesson, I asked my teacher if it was any better. His response was, "Not really."

Since then, I have worked at resonance. The problem is that when we hear resonance within the mouth, the public doesn't hear it. Initially, I began recording my voice. I recall listening to one recording. There was hardly any sound on the recording, while I had heard a very forceful voice when I recorded it. Finally, trusting what I was hearing on the recording, I began to experiment with different options.

An ancient Italian manuscript describes the following method: Inhale through the mouth. At the same time, smell a flower that is in front of the nose.

When we do this, we find that the form of the soft palate and uvula changes when we inhale only through the nose or only through the mouth. Do it. Inhale through the mouth, but at the same time, smell a rose. (To ensure you are including the nose, put your finger in front of your nose with a bit of perfume on your finger. Smell the perfume as you inhale.) We now have a feeling of a triangle inside the mouth, not a rectangle. The tongue is wide and lowered in the back. The soft palate is not wide; it is a point above. We have the shape of a triangle. The uvula is down. The space is behind the uvula, between the uvula and the pharynx, not in front of the soft palate and uvula. Think of this back space as the shape of an egg, narrower at the top and wider at the bottom. Maintain that space while singing. (This paragraph is very dense and presents many new ideas. Work through this paragraph multiple times.)

What we are learning to do is to tune the vocal tract. We should not feel any pressure or tension within the tract. Play with the space. Make it wide, a rectangle, and feel the tension. Return to the feeling of the triangle. The space is vertical. This space is basic in creating a voice that feels easy. The pitch is in tune, and at the same time, the voice projects. Again, repeat the process. Habits are meant to be broken. Rome was not built in a day.

Exercises

1. Inhale through the mouth, but smell that flower. Execute a siren, maintaining that shape. This is a new space.
2. As you are inhaling and smelling a flower, use the Alexander Technique, moving the spine a bit back. Inhale, exhale without changing the space. Sing.
3. Make sure the tongue stays in contact with the front teeth and the molars. At the back of the molars, the tongue is wider.
4. For more projection of the voice, try this:
   a. Raise a finger in front of the nose, inhale to that finger, and then sing to the finger.
   b. Extend your finger to arm's length, inhale to that finger, and then sing to the finger.
   c. Choose a point as far away from you as you can, inhale to that point, and sing to that point.

Note how the support system changes as you change the distance of the projection. Note how the sound changes.

In the following two figures, the top illustration is correct. The mouth is oval. In the bottom figure, the mouth is more closed. Note the difference in the space between the tongue and uvula and soft palate in the two figures. Note that the red part is where there is air and, as a result, space for resonance.

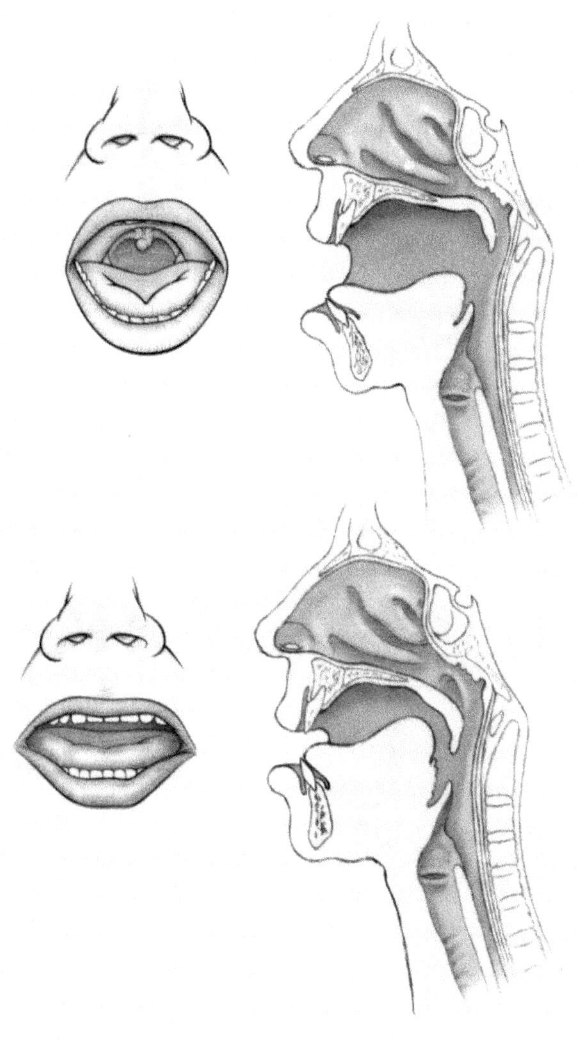

Chapter 7

The Soft Palate

Today in Italy, the soft palate is not often mentioned in the teaching of singing. In the USA and Latin America, it is taught in many different ways. Raise the cheekbones, feel an inside smile, and many more directives are given that often conflict with each other. I have tried all of these methods with my students in the past.

Most of us have been taught the importance of raising and widening the soft palate. This movement of the soft palate gives the singer a feeling of space in the upper part of the mouth, and we think that more space is better. We have a cavern inside. More space means more resonance. No, this isn't true.

I find the Italian method to be the most helpful. The form at the upper back of the mouth is not a rectangle; it is a triangle, the tip of the triangle being at the top. The space needs to be in tune with the pitch.

First, let's again find the soft palate. Touch the tip of the tongue to the upper front teeth. Move the tongue back along the hard palate. Keep moving the tongue back. We hear and feel a click as the tongue and soft palate meet. At the back, attached to the soft palate, is the uvula, that little extension hanging down that we see when we look into our mouths.

The ideal inside form is an inverted V, or this form (ʌ). The tongue is wide at the bottom, and the soft palate is the point at the top. It feels like a triangle inside the mouth rather than a rectangle. The sides of the triangle are relaxed, like curtains hanging down. The uvula is lowered within the triangle.

The antique Italian method of finding resonance by smelling a flower while inhaling through the mouth will give you the correct sensation. (That is covered more completely in Chapter 6.) A very narrow sensation behind the nose is also correct. Any sensation that widens will be wrong. Keeping the oval lip form is important.

Exercise

We do not make the correct space by widening the soft palate. The useful space for resonance is behind the uvula, between the pharynx and the uvula. Sing a pitch with this form, then widen the palate and repeat. You hear a very different sound inside your mouth. It is a good idea to record your voice singing with both methods. What is the difference in sound you hear on the recording? (Just use your cellular device to record.)

Chapter 8

The Pharynx

The pharynx is the back wall of the mouth. It extends from behind the larynx all the way up to behind and above the soft palate. It is unmovable by itself. It is simply a wall. Our only option for moving it is to move the spine, which is behind it.

The two parts of the Alexander Technique that are most useful for singers are the expansion of the ribs, the upper back, and the backward movement of the spine as it connects to the cranium. (The expansion of the ribs is discussed in Chapters 1 and 2.) The second part deals with the movement of the spine. As the spine moves a bit to the back, the head raises. We get a little taller. At the same time, the head tilts down a bit. (You might want to look into this technique more in-depth on the internet.)

As the spine moves slightly back, there is more space between the vocal chords and the pharynx. The fundamental tone is somewhat more secure and fuller. There is also more space behind the uvula. Remember the space for the egg behind the uvula that was mentioned in Chapter 6. Be careful not to raise the placement of the fundamental. The tongue remains flat.

Exercises

1. Sing a pitch, just the fundamental "uh," without the backward movement of the spine. Now sing the same pitch with the spine moved back, maintaining the "uh." Repeat, first relaxed, then while holding the same pitch, move your spine back. This movement creates more space between the larynx and the pharynx. There is also a bit more space between the uvula and the pharynx. The sound and feel will be different.

2. Record yourself, alternating between the backward movement of the spine and the relaxed position, always singing "uh." Repeat, repeat, repeat. These are new muscles, and repetition is essential.
3. Dancers use the idea of a string attached to the top of the head, lengthening the spine. This is also useful for a singer.

Chapter 9

Registrations or Passaggios of the Voice

It is important to recognize the registration changes, or passaggios in the voice. In reality, the vocal chords do change how they function when we sing in the chest voice, middle voice for women, head voice for all, and falsetto for men. It is helpful to deal with those changes positively rather than ignoring them and hoping they will go away.

The passaggio for men, and the lower passaggio for women, is in the area of D flat to F sharp, right above middle C on the piano. Women have a second passaggio about an octave above, D flat to F sharp.

As we work on these transitions, be sure to maintain an open chest, the fundamental form in the larynx, and the free pharynx. Without a correct structure, the breaks will remain obvious.

I have found that the most useful way of working on these transitions is with the glissando. The vowel is an uh [ʌ]. As in Chapter 3 of this book, begin with the vocal fry, followed by the "monster voice," then do a siren up and down, making sure you can always see the uvula at the back of the mouth. Now begin the siren low in the voice and continue through to the top register. Men should include the falsetto. If there are breaks in the voice, try for more space in front of the pharynx by moving the spine back. Do it again, always having a feeling of space in front of the pharynx. Always include the hook space or the nasal pharynx above the soft palate. Do not push the air.

Do the siren with an [ɑ]. As the pitch changes, so must the quality of the [ɑ]. This is called migration of the vowel. The tongue and the space must change gradually as we raise and lower the pitch. The quality of the vowel must also change. Do not hold on to the vowel. Allow the jaw to drop a bit. Nothing is rigid. There should be no feeling of tension or pressure.

The healthiest way to deal with changes of registration is to think of each pitch and vowel as having its own particular registration. Do not hold onto a space or tongue position. If you feel tension, MOVE SOMETHING. Allow the quality of the vowel to change. Allow the quality of the sound to change. As the pitch rises, the head voice becomes more dominant. As the pitch lowers, the chest voice is more dominant. We sing with a mix of the two registers most of the time. A popular singer will generally use more of the chest register higher than a lyric singer. Broadway singers can also choose the mix of registers they need. Their show character will aid in their choices.

The chest voice and the head voice each have their own particular quality when isolated. The chest voice has power. We have a feeling of strength in the voice when we use only that register. The head voice has beauty and resonance. By mixing the registers, each pitch has power and resonance.

Most men have the addition of the falsetto. By working with the siren or glissando, men can connect this register to the head voice without a break. Maintaining the inside form and support is crucial. This registration is essential for a popular singer. Achieving this might take some time.

Women don't have a falsetto. The very light sound some female popular singers switch to is an isolated head voice.

Exercises

1. Begin with a low pitch with just chest registration. Now move the tongue a bit more forward, keeping the back part of the tongue low, and lower the jaw a bit. By moving the tongue and jaw, we have added a bit of the head register to the sound. It is a good idea to record and listen to these two different sounds.
2. Begin with only the light head registration. Gradually add the fundamental pitch by moving the spine backward. This movement introduces the chest registration or fundamental to the sound. Maintain the head registration. Now we have a mixed registration. Record these two sounds. Listen to them.

3. Go back to the siren, beginning low and chesty. As the pitch ascends, keep moving the pharynx back and the tongue forward. Men, continue through the falsetto. Repeat, record, and listen. Always allow for movement of the tongue, the pharynx, and the uvula.

Chapter 10

Exercises for Melding the Registers

The exercises for connecting the registers are all based on the glissando. As the pitch raises and lowers, it is essential to maintain a feeling of flexibility in the vocal tract. The quality will be more chesty with low pitches and more heady with the upper pitches. Allow these changes. The flexibility includes not only the pitch but also the vowel. The vowel quality needs to migrate. The vowel remains, but the quality changes. As the pitch ascends and the jaw lowers, the vowel opens or migrates. The sound of the vowel inside the mouth changes, but the vowel in front of the mouth has the correct sound.

The beginning exercise is always the siren, which we have done numerous times. Establish the fundamental, the spine moves back, there is space in front of the pharynx, and the triangular form is established inside the back of the mouth. The tongue is wide, low in the back, touching the front teeth and molars. The jaw lowers a bit naturally, and the mouth has an oval shape. If you have repeated this form sufficiently while silently inhaling and exhaling, it should by now be a habit. This is called muscle memory.

Singing the [ɑ] vowel, begin on a C and change to a G above. Connect the two pitches by using a portamento or glissando. This is an interval of a fifth. Try it a number of times, not permitting change, then permitting change. Record and listen. Continue the pattern of the interval of a fifth, raising the pitch by half steps. Repeat the interval through the middle range until E or F for the upper note. This is an octave above middle C for women, directly above middle C for men, no higher. Begin the pattern lower if you like. Always allow the jaw to lower and the vowel migrate.

Now change the vowel to [ɔ] and do the same sequence. Always begin in a comfortable range, raising by half steps until the E or F above.

Change the vowel to [i]. This vowel has different challenges, as the tongue on the sides raises to touch the upper molars. If the [i] doesn't project, try this exercise: round the mouth, begin with a spoken [ʌ], and without moving the jaw, move the tongue to an [i]. Repeat, repeat, repeat until the tongue moves sufficiently to the front. The migration of the [i] will be more evident than with the [ɑ] or the [ɔ].

Do the preceding exercises, changing the interval to an octave. The wider the interval the more the space needed to change, while the vowel needs to continue to migrate.

Let's go back to using a siren. As we connect to the head voice for women and, for men, the falsetto, the nasal pharynx will need to engage more. (Feel that the pharynx behind the palate arches a bit up to the front as the tongue moves a bit forward. This is the nasal pharynx.) The transition to the head voice and falsetto needs to be easy and fluid. This is particularly useful for popular singers. The "break" between the head voice and falsetto for men will begin to smooth out.

We are now in control of the quality we want. A popular or Broadway singer may choose a different quality than a classical singer, but the technique is the same.

High sopranos need to maintain a bit of the chest register in the middle and low voice. Without that, many of the arias of Mozart are impossible. The pitch A below middle C is impossible without some connection to the chest register.

In Video 19 on YouTube under Kathryn Kasper or kaspervocalmethod I present a series of vocalizations. These are useful in the connection of the registers and for daily warm-ups.

Chapter 11

Space of the Vocal Tract and the Fundamental Sound

In previous chapters, I have covered what I refer to as the fundamental sound. It is the sound created at the level of the vocal chords. Some pedagogues have referred to this as the cord of nature. All the harmonics of the tone are equal in quality and amplitude. As the voice passes through the vocal tract, certain harmonics are augmented, and others are dampened. (For instance, when we hear an oboe, we recognize the instrument because of the harmonics that are strengthened and dampened within its vocal tract.) The voice is a bit different because of the flexibility of the vocal tract. Each person has their own particular space and quality.

This fundamental tone is easiest to isolate by using the Alexander Technique, moving the spine a bit back, which at the same time moves the pharynx back. After doing this, we have a bit more space behind the larynx and soft palate. At the same time, elongate the spine a bit, moving the head up while keeping the chin level, not raised. Begin the pitch at this level, low within the larynx.

The tongue remains low in the back, touching the lower teeth in the front and the molars on the sides. Beginning with a vocal fry, open the throat by widening the tongue and execute a siren up and down. The vowel is an [ʌ].

The muscle memory at the level of the larynx, the space created by the back position of the pharynx, the tongue, and the oval mouth are all crucial. This may seem like a very complicated coordination, but learned step by step is learnable and easy to memorize.

Now let's change to a vowel. Begin by singing the fundamental on an [ʌ] and change to an [ɑ] without changing the pitch. Repeat the two sounds back and forth, keeping the space between the pharynx and the uvula, and between the pharynx and the larynx.

Begin by singing the fundamental and change the [ʌ] to an [ɔ]. Repeat the two sounds, keeping the space in front of the pharynx.

Begin by singing the fundamental and change the [ʌ] to an [i]. Repeat the process.

Of these three vowels, the [i] is perhaps the most difficult because of the greater movement of the tongue. If the tongue doesn't move sufficiently to the front, the sound will remain inside the mouth. Simply by repeating the tongue movement between an [ʌ] and an [i] until the tongue relaxes in the movement, we can achieve an easy [i]. Another aspect of all vowels is the rounded shape of the lips.

Do not push the sound to the front. Allow the vowel to project the sound. Do not push it against the hard palate. The vowel needs to project directly out of the mouth, together with the connection to the space created by the smelling of a flower.

The memory of the muscles is essential in learning a technique, whether it is singing or a sport. Repetition is essential.

Refer back to the illustration at the end of Chapter 6.

Chapter 12

Recap of the Fundamental

I would like to examine a bit more the idea of the fundamental, the core in the voice, or the first harmonic. All refer to the source of the sound. The initial sound. The cord of nature. The sound that comes directly off the vocal folds or chords. At this level, all the harmonics are equal. When that sound moves through the vocal tract, some of the harmonics are augmented, and others are dampened. The form of each individual vocal tract determines the resulting sound.

To find the fundamental, the throat needs to be open and the larynx a bit lowered. This form is secured by touching the Adams apple with a finger, then swallowing and inhaling simultaneously. (See Chapter 3.) Maintain this space while breathing in and out without sound. Using the Alexander Technique, move the spine back and up with the head raised. At the same time, the pharynx will move a bit back, creating more space behind the larynx. Begin with a vocal fry. Next, open the throat by widening the tongue. Now the sound changes into more of a monster voice. Raise and lower the pitch by executing the sound of a siren. Raise the voice as high and as low as comfortable. It is a glissando. Repeat. Do not permit the space to change. Keep the fundamental and the space.

Begin with a pitch in an easy range, maintaining the open position in the throat. Do not push the sound to the front. Allow it to remain in the back. The vowel will be a schwa or [ʌ]. Rounding the lips a bit more, change to a vowel, to an [ɔ]. The air and pitch are now passing through the lips. Repeat [ʌ], [ɔ], pressing the front of the tongue more firmly against the front lower teeth as you move to the vowel. You now have the second harmonic, or the projection of the voice. Note that the sound passes the hard palate; it doesn't touch it.

Do the same process for the [i] and the [ɑ]. It is a good idea to record the sound you are getting to solidify the muscle memory as you change the structure for the vowel.

Let's go back to the open throat. The tongue is wide, connected to the larynx via muscles. Think of those muscles as points of connection. It might be useful to feel these as two short vertical rods that connect the tongue and the larynx. The area is not rigid.

The oral pharynx is the space we see when looking into the open mouth. We should always be able to see the back of the mouth when doing a siren, with the exception of the [i].

The nasal pharynx is flexible. The pharynx is rather vertical until it reaches the nasal cavity. At this point, it arches to the front as the spine connects to the cranium. By lowering the uvula, we can feel that opening and space. Many teachers refer to this as "covering" and recommend using it when singing higher pitches, especially for men. What if we all include this area when we sing in the lower registers, also? We don't need to change anything in the vocal tract, no matter what pitch we are singing. The support changes to change the pitch. When we inhale, we establish this space along with the space behind the larynx, back of the mouth, and uvula.

In Chapter 3, I talked about the old Italian inhalation with the mouth, but smelling a flower at the same time. This changes the form of the soft palate into an inverted V. The top is a point, creating the space of a triangle (ʌ). The tongue is at the bottom of the triangle, and the soft palate is the tip above. The sides are relaxed and hanging down. The uvula is down within the triangle.

This space is very different from that which we achieve when thinking of raising the palate, creating an inside smile, or raising the cheekbones. With that technique, the space is spread, more of a rectangle. The tongue is pulled back and tense, and the mouth is wider. (I taught these techniques for many years. It feels like there is more space, and more space should result in more resonance, but that isn't the case.)

Now, let us go back to the fundamental sound. Using the Alexander Technique, move the spine back. Establish the two points of connection between the tongue and the larynx. The tongue is wide and touching the front lower teeth. Inhale, including the smell of a flower. This creates a triangle in the back of the mouth. Now sing one note. Repeat with a short breath in between. This onset exercise is very useful. I learned of it from the book by Richard Miller. Repeat. One note, inhale, the same note, inhale, etc., always keeping the structure correct.

Always maintain the feeling of space in front of the pharynx. (Remember the space for the egg.) This space includes the laryngeal pharynx, the oral pharynx, and the nasal pharynx. The space at the level of the oral pharynx is between the pharynx and the soft palate and uvula. It is not in front of the soft palate and uvula. Any feeling of tension or pressure should be eliminated.

Chapter 13

The Fundamental and Projection of the Voice

The fundamental, or the core of the voice, is the sound that is created at the level of the chords. If we feel the pitch begins above this level, the harmonics and projection of the voice will be dampened. For instance, if I hear the first sound at the level of the soft palate or the hard palate, I am not singing with the fundamental.

The feeling in the larynx should not be tense nor relaxed. It should have a feeling of openness. Muscles are being engaged. The connection between the tongue and the larynx should feel secure. Remember to engage those two points, the vertical muscles that connect these two entities. The tongue is wide and flat, but is not pushed down. The tongue does not push down the larynx. The two are connected via muscles that separate them.

The projection of the voice is through the vowels and consonants. I will call this the second harmonic. We don't push the voice out. The words project, creating the second harmonic. Words are produced with the tongue, jaw, and lips, not the throat.

It is useful to do what I call a pretend. Let's use the first words in the Handel aria *Ombra mai fu* to learn this technique. Without any sound, form the words with the lips and tongue, being careful to keep the space for the fundamental, the egg shape, and the triangle in the back. There should be no air sound or whisper. Now say the words with the monster voice, the extension of the vocal fry. The words should be in front of the lips. Now sing the phrase *Ombra mai fu.* If the words don't pass the lips, the support isn't strong enough. (Go back to Chapters 1 and 2.) Open the ribs in the back and sides while raising the abdominals above the belly button. If you don't know the aria *Ombra mai fu,* do the exercise with just the first phrase of any song you choose.

Exercises

1. Sing a phrase, then repeat it. If the words are still not projected, place your index fingers on each side of the rounded lips. Repeat the phrase. The words should be in front of the lips.
2. Rest the palms of your hands on your cheeks, fingers extended to the back, away from the ears. Repeat the phrase. It will be useful to record the results of these steps, as the voice will sound very different from the sound you are accustomed to hearing inside the mouth. Inside the mouth, we hear through the Eustachian tubes. We need to learn to hear the sound through our outer ears.

Chapter 14

Legato Singing

The connection between the air and the vocal sound is critical when attempting to sing a legato line. The glissando (portamento) is the best exercise to use in order to accomplish this.

In an easy range, sing the interval of a fifth. Use the vowel [ɑ]. Do to Sol. Begin on the Do and with a glissando raise to the Sol, followed by the lower Do. Transpose a half step up. Again, Do, Sol, Do. Repeat, transposing the interval a half step at a time, always connecting with the glissando. (It might be useful to begin with a siren, beginning at the bottom of the register, to the top, and again to the bottom. I have talked about the siren earlier in the book.) Repeat, repeat. The tongue should not move up and down while singing the pattern. The throat should remain open. In fact, as we raise the pitch, a feeling of more space in front of the pharynx, back of the uvula, and above the soft palate is useful. Look into your mouth while singing. The uvula should stay in view.

When the interval of the fifth is relatively easy to perform, change to an octave. Do to Do, raising and lowering the pattern by half steps. Again, use the vowel [ɑ].

The next step is singing a simple melody on an [ɑ]. For example, sing the first phrase of the Arie Antiche, *Caro mio ben,* without words. Feel the pitch and the tone pass your lips. Any song will do, only the first phrase. For instance, *Fly Me to the Moon.* Repeat.

Now form the words using the tongue and lips. Make no sound, no whisper. Feel the triangle form in the back. Maintain space in front of the pharynx. *Caro mio ben, Fly me to the moon.* (If you don't know these songs, do the exercise singing any song you choose.)

Sing the vocal line with words. The words should not resonate against the hard palate. They must pass the lips. Use this technique with any song you know, popular or lyrical. The most important thing is not to hear the text inside the mouth. Only when the words pass the lips will the audience understand them. When we hear the words inside, we are raising the tongue and flattening the soft palate.

Use the exercise from Chapter 6, breathing for different distances and singing to that distance.

Chapter 15

Phonetics

This chapter is basically an introduction to the **International Phonetic Alphabet**. (IPA) In this system every sound has a symbol. I am including only those symbols found in the English language. First let's look at the consonants. There are two different types of consonants, those that use the voice and those that use only air. The two consonant sounds in the same line have the same form in the tongue, lips and palate. First there is a list of the most used consonants under two headings, **vocalized** and **only air,** followed by singular sounds, liquids, diphthongs and finally vowel sounds. Since some of the symbols will be new to many of you, I will include a common English word using that sound.

Consonants

Vocalized

[ð] t̲h̲e
[b] best
[d] d̲og
[v] v̲ery
[g] g̲ood
[z] z̲ero
[ʒ] garag̲e, az̲ure
[dʒ] j̲ud̲g̲e

Only air

[θ] t̲h̲ink
[p] put
[t] t̲alk
[f] f̲ish
[k] k̲ind
[s] s̲oon
[ʃ] s̲h̲ut
[tʃ] c̲h̲ur̲c̲h̲
[ks] so c̲k̲s̲
[h] h̲e

[ŋ] si<u>ng</u>
[ɲ] ca<u>ny</u>on
[ɝ] h<u>ear</u>d - sing on the r, country western
[ɜ] h<u>ear</u>d - open the vowel - little coloring of the r

Liquids

[l] look
[m] much
[n] nice
[r] rich

Diphthongs – The first vowel is the dominant sound except when singing Country Western. The exception is the [ju] - we sing on the [u]

[aI] - my
[ɔI] - boy
[ƐI] - bait
[ju] - you
[oU] - boat
[ɑU] – ouch

Vowel Sounds

[ɑ] calm
[i] beet
[I] bit
[Ɛ] let
[o] obey - closed vowel, not often used while singing
[ɔ] aught - open o - lips rounded, open and extended a bit
[u] too

[U] took
[ʌ] up - in accented positions
[ə] above - schwa - in unaccented positions
[æ] cat

The projection of the words is basic for singing as the text tells the story of the song. When I was in college the choir director would say "diction, diction". What I did was counterproductive as I sang the word more distinctly for myself to hear. If we hear the words clearly inside the mouth, they are not clear for the public. The words have to pass the lips in order for the public to understand them.

Another example from the past: I was performing the Aaron Copland songs with the texts by Emily Dickinson. I love her poems and the cycle is favorite of mine. I tried very hard to enunciate the poems well. After the performance I asked a friend if she understood the texts and she said "Not really". I heard the words very distinctly. What was wrong? I was hearing them through my Eustachian tubes which connect the back of the throat to the middle ear. The words were not passing my lips. The less distinctly we hear the words as we sing the better the public will hear them.

Chapter 16

Muscle Memory

Singing is a sport, or at least we need to adopt habits from sports players. It is the boring or challenging part. It is the repetition of the same sequence of events until we get it right. How many times will a basketball player practice the free throw? 1,000, 10,000? Maybe more. A soccer player repeats a kick until the ball goes exactly where he wants it to go. A skater does the same, as does every sports player. We have to pattern ourselves after sports. Repeat, repeat. Then we remember which muscles to use while we sing and which not to use.

The entire physical structure is involved. Let's begin with the diaphragm. When we inhale, the rib cage expands. To begin singing, we raise the abdominals above the belly button. (If you need a refresher, go back to Chapters 1 and 2.)

The larynx needs to maintain a feeling of openness while singing. We do this by using muscles. This openness is created with the muscles between the tongue, larynx, and the pharynx.

First, the tongue. It touches behind the lower front teeth when at rest, widening to the molars, and behind the molars, it widens further.

The tongue is attached to the larynx with muscles. Think of those muscles as two "pins" or points of connection between the tongue and the larynx. The tongue and the larynx are connected via these "pins."

Within the larynx, we have the true vocal folds and above them the false vocal chords. These false vocal chords have nothing to do with singing, and we must be careful not to engage them when singing or talking. We use them when we cough and when we go to the bathroom. They hyper-tense the vocal folds. To feel them, begin a cough. Feel the soft tissue closing the larynx. These muscles, or tissues, are the false vocal chords. Notice that when you engage them, the tongue dips in the middle. For this reason, it is best to maintain a feeling that the tongue is flat and wide while singing. Some popular singers use the false vocal chords to create a sort of "dirty" sound. Be careful while doing this. Try to use that sound only occasionally.

We create a bit more space in front of the pharynx by using the Alexander Technique, moving the spine a bit back, raising the top of the head, and tilting the head a bit down. This new space includes the laryngo pharynx, the oral pharynx, and the nasal pharynx.

To achieve the correct space in front of the pharynx, inhale with the mouth, but smell a flower at the same time. (Recall the old Italian method for resonance.) The form above in the back is a $\wedge$, not a rectangle. The soft palate is a point at the top. The sides are like curtains hanging down. At the bottom is the tongue, completing a triangle.

All of these movements use muscles. They are very specific muscles. By repeating the exercises, it will become easier to select the correct muscles while performing. A feeling of openness without pressure or tension is our goal.

Richard Miller, in his book The Structure of Singing, suggested using what he called the Onset Exercise. Simply repeat any vowel on a pitch. Sing one note, inhale, sing it again. This is a very useful exercise. Repeat until the muscles that form the space are secure. We can also do this without sound. I call it a pretend. Repeat until the muscle memory is secure.

Chapter 17

Melisma, Interpolation and Runs

Popular and classical singers execute melodies with melisma or interpolation. Melisma or interpolation is the ornamentation of the melody of a song. Many times in popular music, the changes are high in the register. Classical or lyric singers use melisma, especially with arias from the Baroque period. After that time, most of the melisma was written out by the composers.

Cecilia Bartoli became very well known outside of Italy when she produced a recording of Arie Antiche with a lot of ornamentation. Her melisma was very staccato, pulsed with the diaphragm. That is one option. It isn't wrong.

Another option is maintaining the structure in the vocal tract that I have been discussing in this book while executing a legato pattern. Allow the tones to change rapidly within the space, keeping the air pressure solid but not pushed. Do not allow the fundamental to change its position while doing this. In my experience using this technique, the pitches are more in tune, and the lines are smoother.

A vocalise book that is very helpful for singers of all levels is the Vaccai Vocal Method. It is available in various keys. The first seven exercises cover the intervals from the second to the octave. The rest of the book is an introduction to the Baroque ornaments with the addition of runs and trills. It is available on Amazon. By applying those standard ornaments to songs, the expression of the text is enhanced.

The Metropolitan Opera in New York City has been regularly offering the operas of Handel. The standard aria form from this period is the da capo aria, ABA. The first section is repeated with ornaments. Some classical singers, for example, Joyce DiDonato, have become masters of this craft.

Popular singers, especially those with a black church tradition, use the same ideas.

Whatever the style, maintain the space in front of the pharynx with the ribs and back open. This helps to eliminate the pushing of the air. Agility is what is required, no matter the vocal style.

Chapter 18

Sing: Practical Ways of Learning and Teaching

There are two schools of thought for teaching and learning to sing. The empirical school deals with how the voice feels and sounds. We learn by doing. The second school is based more on an anatomical model. The anatomy of the thorax and vocal tract are the basis of this school. In this book, I use a mix of the two schools.

Before William Vennard published in 1967 "Singing: The Mechanism and Technic", the majority of vocal teaching was empirical. To this day, I find the anatomical illustrations in this book the most useful for teaching and learning. They are "stripped away" illustrations, showing only what is essential. There are three illustrations that are very useful: the thorax, the larynx, and the tongue. (I find knowing all the muscles to be superfluous.)

In 1987, Richard Miller published "The Structure of Singing", going much further toward the anatomical model. The text is dense. (I do use his "onset" exercise regularly.)

In the 1990s, Joan Wall and Robert Caldwell published a series of videos illustrating the anatomy of the voice, "The Singer's Voice".

Early in the 21st century, Theodore Dimon published a book for singers and vocal therapists with very dense illustrations, "Anatomy of the Voice". All of these books, and many more I have not cited, push the learning of singing toward the anatomical model.

I feel there is a need to move back in the direction of the empirical model. I am very thankful for the Vennard illustrations and some thoughts from the other books, but is knowing facts a way to teach voice? Singers need to learn to use muscles, to use the correct muscles. We need to learn to feel. If we feel pressure or tension in the larynx or vocal tract, we need to be able to solve the problem empirically. The structure inside that tract is complex, but is it really important for a singer to know all the correct names of all the parts?

Chapter 19

Special Issues

Some people have a difficult time matching a pitch. For most, there is a solution. The problem usually has to do with the connection between the air and the pitch. The lip trill is the most useful exercise for connecting the two. When we were children and played with toy cars and trucks, we did a lip trill for the sound of the toy. It's the same sound. Do it while making a sound with the voice, up and down. Choose a pitch on an instrument and try to match it with a lip trill. Try a short melody, for example, the first phrase of Happy Birthday. The lip trill is also very useful for warming up the voice.

Many singers have trouble singing in tune, especially in the upper register. We think it takes more air to sing high, so we pressure the air. It doesn't take more air to sing high. It only takes more support. This added air causes the throat to close and, as a result, the pitch is out of tune. The singer generally feels tension or pressure. Opening the ribs in the back as the pitch ascends will help. Move the tongue and alter the space inside. MOVE. Don't be afraid to move. Apply the information we have already learned.

Observations on the vibrato. If you hear your vibrato in the throat while singing, the vibrato will be too fast if you are young, too slow if you are older, or too dominant. Open the throat and remain open, and the vibrato will be natural, not dominant. You will need to record yourself to gain trust in this method.

If you have problems with TMJ and opening your mouth hurts, try this. Touch the sides of your face in front of the ears with the index fingers at the indentation. Open your mouth a bit, maintaining the oval form. This might aid in singing without pain in that joint. Breathe in and out. Try a glissando. Touching that indentation also helps maintain the correct form of the soft palate and uvula while singing.

Many pedagogues encourage men to "cover" the voice as they sing to the top of their register. This is the connection of the nasal pharynx to the sound. I would like to suggest that both men and women include this sound in all of the registers. As we move the spine a little back, include the space back of and above the soft palate. At the connection of the spine to the cranium, the space moves to the front. Think of it as a hook. If we always include this space when we sing, the upper range becomes easier and more in tune.

I would like to thank each of you for working through this book. Many of the ideas presented here are new; some are old. I hope that you continue to study your voice and learn better how to use it. Incorporate as much as you see fit from this book into your daily practice. My hope is that you have found the book useful. My best to all of you.

Continue to follow my videos on YouTube, Kathryn Kasper, or kaspervocalmethod.